A Visit to
ITALY

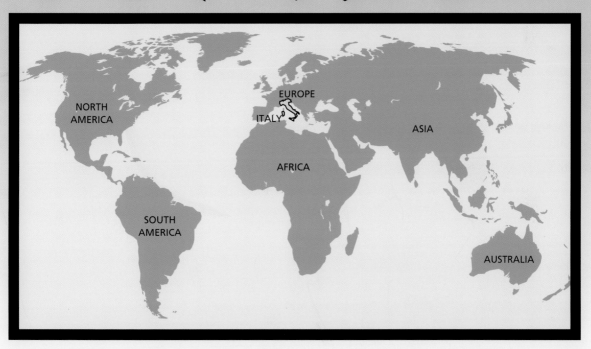

NORTH
AMERICA

EUROPE

ITALY

ASIA

AFRICA

SOUTH
AMERICA

AUSTRALIA

Rachael Bell

Heinemann
LIBRARY

First published in Great Britain by Heinemann Library,
Halley Court, Jordan Hill, Oxford OX2 8EJ
a division of Reed Educational and Professional Publishing Ltd.

Heinemann is a registered trademark of Reed Educational & Professional Publishing Ltd.

OXFORD   MELBOURNE   AUCKLAND
JOHANNESBURG   BLANTYRE   GABORONE
IBADAN   PORTSMOUTH (NH) USA   CHICAGO

Designed by AMR
Illustrations by Art Construction
Printed in Hong Kong/China

03 02 01 00 99
10 9 8 7 6 5 4 3 2 1

ISBN 0 431 08342 8

British Library Cataloguing in Publication Data

Bell, Rachael
  A visit to Italy
  1. Italy – Juvenile literature
  I.Title II.Italy
  945

Acknowledgements

The Publishers would like to thank the following for permission to reproduce photographs:
Axel Poignant Archive, (Ali Reale) p. 29; Colorific, (David Levenson/Black Star) p. 22;
Colorsport, p. 24; Hutchison Library, (J Davey) p. 23; (Isabella Tree) p. 25; J Allan Cash, pp. 9,
17, 21; Katz Pictures, (A Tosatto) p. 14; Performing Arts Library, (Gianfranco Fainello) p. 28;
Robert Francis, p. 18; Robert Harding Picture Library, (Mike Newton) pp. 12, 20; Spectrum
Colour Library, p. 13; Stock Market, p. 10; Telegraph Colour Library, pp. 8; (C Chinca) p. 5;
(J Sims) pp. 6, 16; Tony Stone, (Joe Cornish) p. 11; Trevor Clifford, pp. 12, 16; Trip, (R Cracknell)
p. 7; (P Nicholas) p. 15; (W Jacobs) pp. 20, 26; (H Rogers) p. 27.

Cover photograph reproduced with permission of Telegraph Colour Library (A. Tilley)

Any words appearing in bold, **like this**, are explained in the Glossary.

Contents

Italy

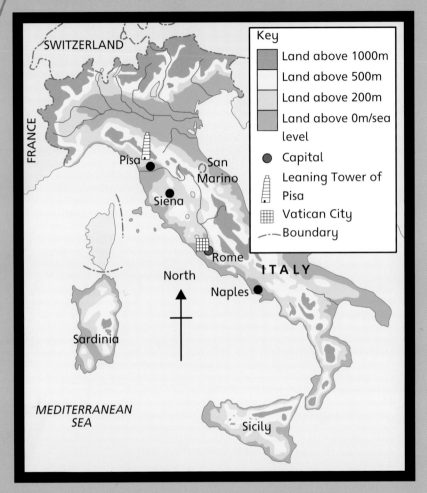

Italy is in southern **Europe**. On a map it looks like a boot sticking out into the Mediterranean Sea. Sicily and Sardinia are islands that are part of Italy.

About 100 years ago, 20 areas joined up to make Italy. There are still two places inside Italy that are not part of it. They are the Vatican City and San Marino.

Land

Most of the land in Italy is mountains or hills. These have only thin soil. Farming is difficult here. Many plants cannot grow in thin soil.

The highest mountains are in the north of Italy. They have snow on them all year round. In the south it is much hotter and there is very little rain.

Landmarks

One of Italy's most famous buildings is the Leaning Tower of Pisa. It is over 800 years old. There are 294 steps to the top!

The Vatican City is like a small, separate town inside Rome. It is the home of the **Pope**. There are lots of beautiful works of art by famous artists here.

Homes

Most people in Italy live in towns or cities. This is the city of Naples. It grew up around a busy **port**. People left the countryside to come here for work.

In the country most houses have a small area of land around them. Here people can grow food for themselves or to sell.

Food

Many families enjoy eating together.
For lunch they might eat cold meats
with salad, **pasta**, bread and cheese.

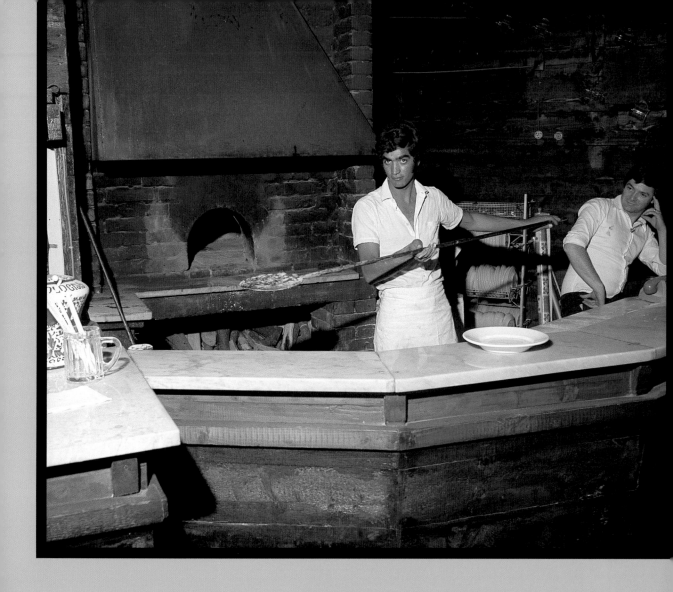

Many delicious foods come from Italy.
Pizzas first came from Naples but now
most towns have a pizzeria. You can
watch the pizzas being made here.

Clothes

Young people wear casual or sports clothes.

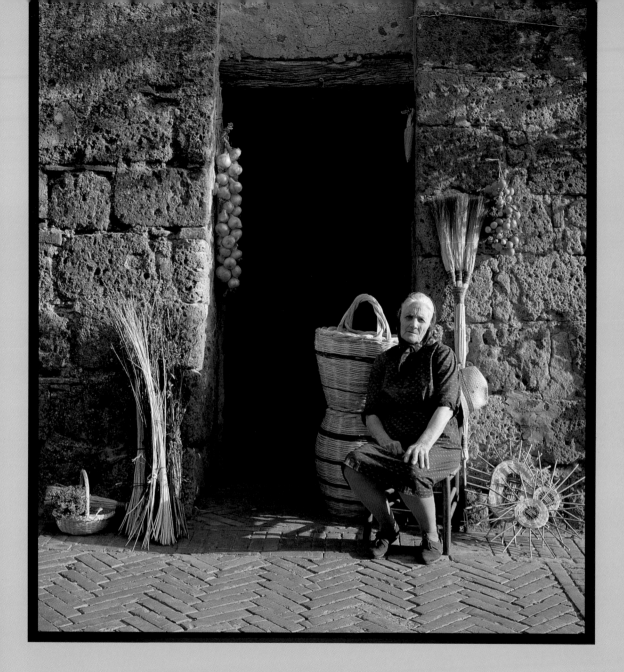

Some of the older people wear black because they are in **mourning**.

Work

Some people work in farming. They grow grapes, wheat, fruit and vegetables. This farm in Sicily is growing oranges.

In central and southern Italy many people work in shops and offices. They close for **siesta** because it is so hot. Most of Italy's **products**, like cars or engines, are made in the north.

17

Transport

Italy has good roads and **toll** motorways.
It also has a very good train service.
There are **ports** and airports too.
Many young people ride **scooters**.

A more unusual transport is the **gondolas** in Venice. You need them to get around this city which has **canals** instead of streets.

Language

Italy's official language is Italian. But different **regions** have their own **dialect**. Italian is based on two old languages.

The other main language is Sardinian.
This is spoken by people on the island of
Sardinia. These Sardinian children are
wearing special clothes for a **procession**.

School

Primary school is for six to eleven year olds. School starts at 8.30 am and finishes at about 1.00 pm. Pupils go to school six days a week.

Middle school is for 11 to 14 year olds. Their day is longer and they usually have sports after school hours. Some pupils go to high school.

Free time

Most Italians love football. People of all ages talk about it and play it. There are big matches on Sunday afternoons.

In the early evening it is usual for people to meet up and walk around the main square or street in their town. This walk is called the 'passeggiata' (pa-se-jarta).

Celebrations

Every town in Italy has at least one festival. People take the day off work or school to watch a **procession** through the town.

On 2 July and 16 August there is a bareback horse race in Siena. Before the race people parade around the main square in costumes.

The Arts

Italy has many **opera** singers and many Italians enjoy opera. Some of the operas take place in the **stadiums** built by the ancient Romans.

The Punch and Judy show comes from the puppet shows that started in Italy hundreds of years ago. Today, puppet shows are still very popular in Sicily.

Factfile

Name	The full name for Italy is the Italian Republic.
Capital	The **capital** of Italy is Rome.
Languages	Italy has two official languages: Italian and Sardinian.
Population	About 58 million people live in Italy.
Money	Italian money is called lira.
Religions	Almost all Italians are brought up as Roman Catholic.
Products	Italy produces wheat, vegetables, olives, wine, machinery and clothes.

Words you can learn

uno (oono)	one
due (do-eh)	two
tre (tray)	three
si (see)	yes
non (noh)	no
buon giorno (bwon jorno)	hello
arrivederci (a-re-va-der-che)	goodbye
per favore (per-faVOR-eh)	please
grazie (grat-zi)	thank you

Glossary

ancient Romans	the people who ruled most of Europe from Rome, over 2000 years ago
canal	a river dug by people
capital	the city where the government is based
dialect	the language spoken by people in one area
Europe	the countries which are north of the Mediterranean Sea
gondola	old-fashioned boat that is used in Venice
mourning	being sad because someone you love has died
pasta	a kind of dough that is made from flour and is cooked in boiling water. Spaghetti is a type of pasta.
opera	a play with music and singing
Pope	the head of the Roman Catholic Church
port	the place where ships pick up and drop off the goods they are carrying
procession	a group of people walking along behind each other and often wearing costumes
product	a thing which is grown, taken from the earth, made by hand or made in a factory
regions	an area or part of a country
scooters	small-wheeled motorbikes
siesta	a time for people to rest or sleep during the middle of the day
stadium	a large sports ground surrounded by seats
toll	a payment you have to make for driving on the motorway

Index